Not Now, Brain.

Lauren Ankers

BookLeaf Publishing

Presentation by *BookLeaf Publishing*

Web: www.bookleafpub.com

E-mail: info@bookleafpub.com

ISBN: 9789357441711

First edition 2023

DEDICATION

For my family and friends who catch me when I fall.

ACKNOWLEDGEMENT

Thank you to all those who have touched my soul.

PREFACE

I have been writing poetry since my mid-teens and it's been a hobby and a crutch simultaneously. Since I have been in mental and substance recovery writing these poems has become my lifeline - I pour my soul into these words.
This is simply a collection of my mind, inside out, for the world to see.

Necrotic Neurosis

Fever kills some while others convalesce
…there is a finale to their distress.
But what of an illness with no expiration?
No cure,
No natural cessation.
No theories, no intrusive tests,
No rashes, no lumps in the breast.
A sickness the eyes cannot find.
Disease loitering within a mind.

Coffee shops or light lunch,
We've met,
Month upon month.
But I have this voice in my head
…words are maliciously said.
Illustrations of cruelty and deceit.
The aim…
The render me obsolete.
Whisper. Stab.
Drive me silently insane.
Coordinate my failures.
Vilify my name.

How can I know truth from deception?
When hearing these hissed preconceptions?
Their voices rattling in my mind
…pitiless, demeaning, and unkind.
The don't care or empathise
Their whispered words are desensitised.

The voices' insolent retorts.
How can I think? How can I talk?

Light is the dark; day becomes night,
The black haze descends,
It holds me tight
I hide under the covers
Unable to rise
Mentally composing
My final goodbyes.
I cry and I sob,
I'm engulfed by despair
Do you see me?
Are you there?
Can you hear my plea?
Please help me!

Do you know my pain?
Can your thoughts entertain?
Something that can't be seen,
Despite my tormented screams.
Can you feel the abyss?
Can you hear the whispered hiss?
Can you see the necrosis?
Of my festering psychosis?

Renegade

I am no-one,
A photon,
A light,
Shining bright.

No definition.
Opus of intuition.
To be defined,
Labels are assigned-

Irregular. Eccentric.
Neurotic. Schizophrenic.
Memorable. Formidable.
Irrational. Unpredictable.

A rhythm maker.
Rule breaker.
Legit not fake,
Create earthquakes

A radical soul
Uncontrolled
Out the fishbowl
Square in a round hole

A renegade.
No masquerade,
No disguise,
Or guise.

Untitled

Seeping from my mind,
Alphabet intertwined,
Weaving like a willow,
Rhythmic words billow.

Thoughts construed,
Verse exudes,
Surging like the sea,
Spewing from my psyche.

Text in my brain,
Ink in my veins,
Onto this scroll,
I bleed my soul.

Homo By Design

There is no definition,
Though many have tried to define,
To place it neatly in a box,
Rather than have something unorthodox.

It's the catching of her eye,
When she passes me by.
It's my heart's palpitation,
When her soul shares my vibration.
There are no conscious selections,
To your antiquated objections,
There's no decision to feel this way,
- It's like breathing day to day.

I'm not troubled with ill or ails.
I didn't wake and choose to like females.
There are no rebellious thoughts,
It's not something I can be taught.
I was born with this characteristic,
It's undeniably naturalistic.

There is no definition,
Though many have tried to define,
There is no imposition
I am homo by design

Just Jane

I tried to rationalise,
Before being psychoanalysed,
Attempts at normalcy,
Made me act abnormally,
Character from another's perspective,
Appears false and deceptive,
Judgement and condemnation,
For a psychological formation.

Shall we argue and debate?
Of the unicorn's tangible state?
Or bake an elderberry pie?
{Who knew it was our final goodbye?}
Let's study antimatter's dimensional force,
And chase the imps who steal our thoughts.
My mind wonders and I think of you,
Are you happy? Living life anew?

Deemed too eccentric,
For being non-concentric,
Synapses run against the grain,
Producing something arcane.
I won't abandon my philosophies,
For generic ideologies,

Denounce this balderdash,
And every artificial eyelash!
- A dream whispered on what is faux,
Will be incomplete and never grow.

Unicorns magic is in their horns,
Antimatter is for when we're reborn.
You'll always have a piece of my heart,
...and I ate the elderberry tart.
I've never forgotten, I'll never forget,
What a ride: no regrets.

I know this is out of the blue,
Just a quick hello, passing through.
I hope you're settled and content?
I hope you live without torment?
"...Do not go gentle into that good night
Rage rage against the dying of the light..."
Maybe one day we'll reunite
Until then, keep shining bright.

Again

There's a feeling in the air:
- Hanging
Like a chord around my stomach:
- Strangling
A taste so bitter:
- Metallic
Reminiscent of something:
- Nostalgic
Of a life once lived:
- Wild child
And of long-gone memories:
- Exiled
To be here in this moment:
- Dejected
For the part of my life:
- Neglected
To be with the masses:
- Mingling
People and wine glasses:
- Ringing
I long for this humdrum:
- Hustle
I want to meet new people:
- Bustle
I feel I am losing:
- Conceding

When I should be out here:
- Succeeding
My world has come to a halt:
- Stagnation
What's different is scary:
- Intimidation
Turn of the page is hard:
- Distressing
Alone, the world:
- Oppressing
Unable to take the next step:
- Blinded
Because I fear the light:
- Misguided
Again, but this time better:
- Progressive
Again, but this time corrected
- Successive
Again, but this time stronger:
- Resilient
Again, but this time thriving:
- Brilliant
Again, but this time prouder:
- Indisputable
Again, but this time:
- Beautiful

Alien

See our diversity,
Nature's complexities.
Human's similitude,
Individualised by attitude.

Humanity's tide,
Far and wide,
Endless projecting,
Endless connecting.

Faces identified,
Names applied,
Many unacquainted,
Ignorance reciprocated.

Lives intertwined,
Previously aligned,
Memories a mirage,
Nostalgia a collage.

One mesmerised,
Beauty visualised,
Passionate desires,
Baptism of fire.

Divisions of race,
United through place,
Parted through nation,
Allied by migration,

Solitary ambitions,
Shared traditions,
Sameness highlighted,
People united.

This civilization,
Earth's generation,
A collection of aliens:
Homo-sapiens.

The Somme

I saw him standing there
Like a silent nightmare
His face reminded me
Of something I couldn't see.

Who are you?
His face a grey hue.
Why are you here?
His eyes began to tear.

Look into my eyes
My dear dear child.
I am your blood
I died in the mud.

I don't know you
What happened to you?
I asked him! I asked him!
He looked at me grim.

Dear girl, I'm your grandad
This is me, just a lad.
I went off to war
My son I never saw.

I sat there aghast
Thinking of the past.
My papa never spoke
Of his dad, that bloke.

Tell me more,
Tell me about the war
I begged, I pleaded
The information I needed.

I died in the Somme:
Day twenty-one
Many thousands fell before
And many thousands more.

At Verdun I fought for my king
I Threw my hat in the ring.
I gave my today
So you would be okay.

The ground was littered.
The ground glittered.
The shimmer of blood.
The death in the mud.

The stagnant trenches,
Full of silent wrenches.
Darkness from the men at my side
It was a muted goodbye.

When that whistle did blow
Over the top I must go.
My fate in the hands
Of the German command.

I ran hard, I ran fast
Many a crater passed
The Boche were in sight
I could see the light!

Through shells I had run
Past the whizzing machine guns
Then they hit me
ONE! TWO! THREE!

I took bullets to the chest
-Into my breast.
One hit my heart
I did instantly depart.

I saw horrors I can't tell
…On them we mustn't dwell.
Many a friend
Met his end.

I gave my today
So you would be okay.
A solemn loss of life
And to think it happened twice!?

Words are stronger than actions
They can solve all fractions.
Lay down the arms.
End these harms!

Lest you forget.
The lesson is set.
Do not forget the 11th of November
A lesson for all to remember.

Possession

YOU! COME CLOSE TO ME!
Hear its whispers.
Listen to its utterings:
-vicious tongue twisters.

There will be annihilation,
Per its hissed commands,
Down in damnation!
With its malevolent demands.

YOU! COME CLOSE TO ME!
It corrupts my intellect.
Watch it manipulate,
My private introspect.

I like the look of you.
I wanna see you pert.
I wanna come with, come too.
'Cos I am a pervert.

YOU! COME CLOSE TO ME!
Look how it infests.
Peer into my eyes,
See my unwanted guest.

A monster lurks within,
Waiting for a break,
Waiting to begin,
Leaving hellfire in its wake.

YOU! COME CLOSE TO ME!
See the war inside,
The internal conflict,
Where it and I reside.

I'll kill you with a cleaver.
Oh, what a bloodbath,
And I'll do it with fever.
'Cos I'm a psychopath.

*

YOU! COME CLOSE TO ME!
Show me how to mend,
Intellectual transgression.
Help me to transcend,
This demonic possession.

The Absolution Of A Broken Soul

1: Confession

Wanton aggression.
Dishonourable cretin.
Wicked indiscretion.

*

Criminality,
and brutality.
Mind infested,
With drugs ingested.

Altercations.
Vilifications.
Deviancy doubled:
“Ah, she’s troubled.”

Contradictions.
Addictions.
Societies tatter
-I don’t matter.

2: Penance

The pit of my gut,

Like a paper cut,
Pulls and heaves,
Stings and bleeds.

Worthless,
Wicked; defected.
Fake and twisted:
My core infected.

Succumb to voices,
In my head,
Is this psychosis?
Or crimes unsaid?

Ambitionless.
Dejected.
Passionless,
And rejected.

Corruption.
Cynical soul.
Destruction.
Takes a heavy toll.

3: Resistance

My Fate?
-transition

I reshape,
My definition.

*

Expiration
Begets decay.
Decomposition
Is underway.

Disintegration.
Putrefaction.
Augmentation.
Reincarnation.

Death,
Begets beginnings.
And new breath,
Into the living.

4: Hope

I reminisce,
Of metamorphosis
From damnation,
A transformation.

I feel.
I embrace.
I heal,
With grace.

I wonder:
Not lost,
Just farther,
From lines crossed.

I search,
This Earth,
For self-worth,
After re-birth.

5: Birth

From shame,
Comes a new name.
Foundations,
From transfigurations.

Deeds acted.
Words spoken.
Sequences.
Eternal, unbroken.

Revolutions,

-birth and death,
Future created,
In every breath.

Lake Windermere

When my heart no longer beats,
Do not bury me beneath your feet,
Let me remain under this moon,
Free from the limits of an eternal tomb.
Turn my body to ashes and dust,
Grant me to her wind's gentle gusts.
Release my ashes where the swans glide.
Leave me flowing with Windermere's tides.
Let me drift with the ebb and flow,
Of the lake's gentle to and fro.
Let me stay with her summer throngs,
Where my heart truly belongs.
Once my mind has undisturbed rest,
Take me to where my soul knows best.
Scatter my ashes on Windermere's beach,
And let me sleep with the swans and geese.
Feel me falling in her rains,
And let me settle on the swans' terrain.
Hear me in her westerly winds,
Here I rest and gain my wings.
Lake Windermere is where I remain,
And with her next flow we shall meet again.

Khoren

Oh, how they took me by surprise,
Those deep brown boundless eyes.
My body like the heart complete,
Skipped an entire protracted beat.
Oh, how I was taken unprepared,
When our eyes that day paired.
It's been so long since I had a connection,
It's been so long since I've seen perfection.
I fear to look into your eyes,
For baring my soul in reply,
To stand so naked for you to see,
Each vice and virtue that makes me, me,
In that glance a story to be told,
In one look I saw a beautiful soul.

Ode To a Piston

Up and down,
Up and down,
The pistons moves up and down,
Turn the crankshaft,
Round and round,
Round it goes,
Spinning quick,
One stroke,
Two stroke,
Three stroke, four,
Turn the wheels,
That kiss the floor,
Spin the belt,
Endless orbits,
POWER TO
THE ALTERNATOR!
Feed the battery,
The power generator,
Spin the belt,
Round and round,
Turn the camshaft,
Spin the lobes,
Make them pound,
On those springs,
That feed the chamber,

With fuel and things,
CHARGE! The distributer,
To fire those plugs,
Burn that fuel,
The pistons hug,
Up and down,
Up and down,
The pistons move,
Up and down,
To turn the crankshaft,
Round and round,
One stroke,
Two stroke,
Three stroke, four,
The engine purrs,
Evermore.

Adam

You know about six degrees of separation
How everyone is connected in graduation
This is true for all who grace earth
Through you, me, and rebirth

I never knew you existed,
Yet we co-existed,
You walked a path I once trode,
That scouting, sixty-second Griffin Road.

Unbeknown to me,
You knew my family,
Clare, Genbob and Skip,
All played a part in your script.

Yesterday you were a photo on Facebook,
But instantly my world was shook.
A connection I can't quite explain,
Crazy, heartfelt, and arcane.

You touched my soul, your story and smile,
You inspired me to walk that extra mile,
Your loss was heartfelt, painful, and real,
Spinning in my head, your final ordeal.

Connect with what brings out the human in you,
And, Adam, for me, that was you.
I will now life my life to its absolute best,
Sleep now my dear, lay at rest.

The Light

The light lives in you,
Can you see? Can you see?
It's there, burning bright,
A lighthouse on the sea,
It shines and shimmers,
Like raindrops on a lea,

Crawl, walk or run,
It's waiting for you there,
Ready to be embraced,
Like the firework mid-air,
Run, run as fast as you can,
And catch it mid-flare.

Reach out and hold on,
The light before your eyes,
What's that you say?
It's a firefly that dies,
With each grasp you give,
It scatters into the skies.

But, no, I tell you,
These little dots so bright,
They sparkle far and wide,
And brighten up your night,

Like a beacon in the dark,
Until you find your light.

Vagabond

If you saw this vagabond,
Would you pause to correspond?
With a vagrant like me.
- A societal absentee.
Would you toss funds at my feet?
Or perhaps offer something to eat

Would you have a conversation?
With this habituated denomination
If I asked as threadbare
To offer me your evening prayer
For some solid foundations
To build upon my aspirations
Would you raise me off the ground?
And help me turn this around
Would you lift this downbeat?
Back onto her tentative feet

I lost my way on this path
And this is the aftermath
A few wrong junctions
And everything malfunctioned
Here I am, down and out
Lost, broken, and washed out

I’m of good soul and consciousness
But I’ve found myself powerless
To offer up any resistance
And turn around my existence

Forever Grey

Lay at your side in this silent room,
Empty,
But for our hushed emotion,
My wrath of how,
You lay stripped you bare,
Of everything you once were,
Builds upon this ache,
Love. Loss.
Enclose your body within mine,
Heeding these fading breaths,
I pray you tremble,
From your love to me,
And not such terminal pain,
Do not fear, my dear,
I am here,
For better and,
The worst,
My whisper of warmth,
A touch, a kiss,
Gentle embrace as you pass,
A cruel coveted release,
In this silent room,
In mournful peace,
I feel you,
Worlds apart,

Your life pulsates,
My living beats,
Here it shall stay,
Within my sorrowful.
Breath of life,
Forever grey.

Stuck In A Rut

How do you get yourself out of a rut?
Like, I've stagnated; I'm stuck.
For six long months,
Still as the Queen's Guard
Sedentary and immobile,
Like a stone, like lard.
My brain's stopped thinking,
Though spinning it is still,
There is no inspiration,
No wanting, no wishing,
No will.
My feet haven't felt,
The pounding of the floor,
For week upon week,
I've barely stepped through the door,
My world's become dull,
Like an empty shade of grey,
But I'm not down and out,
I'm happy; I'm okay!
I'm just stuck in a rut,
Idle and still,
I need space to think,
I need to recharge and refill.

The Can

It was a fine day in the month of June,
Shining sun, clouds wispy and thin,
Each songbird was gracing an uplifting tune.
Harmony with life's yang and yin.

I was walking up a short tree-lined street,
Alone with my thoughts and dreams,
When a friend greeted and walked to my beat,
She looked troubled, her mind at unease.

I questioned, "Why is it you look so glum?"
She replied with an answer in spoken code,
"I am afraid of some things which have now begun,
A journey I must take down an unknown road."

I asked "Why do you fear the route of chance?
And why fret at the opportunity to move along?"
She answered "I cannot see my future at a glance,
It's all I know, this dance to life's song,
It's time to move on and walk away,
I must move with my hearts desired flow,
Leave my home, routines, and day to day,
But I fear what lies ahead and where I will go."

I mused for a little and replied,
"You should not be afraid of moving on,
Many have done this, prospered, and survived,
It's the only way to reach the place you
belong…

Try to see your life as a soda pop can"
She shrieked "You can't compare life to a can of
fizz!"
"This is true" I replied, "Metal is not such as
man,
But it's the inners that count; listen to this:

"Imagine your life to be that can of pop,
First its full of flavour and sparkling fizz,
In time you drink till the very last drop,
That juice is the place where you live."

"This is your home and these your friends,
But compare it to life and where in it you stand.
You've drunk the juice, the tastes at its end,
And you stand with the empty can in your
hand."

"The can is of no use to your future years,
You discard it without a thought,
Like your existence and the life, you have here;
Move on; a new can being sought."

She said “It’s time to let go now the flavour has gone,
I must go and find a new sparking place.”
“Yes” I replied, “this is the only way to get along.
Discover somewhere new, find a new drink to taste.”

Ten Years

How much evolution,
Goes in life's revolution,
Of ten years:
Three thousand, six hundred and forty-eight
days.
That's one hundred and twenty Fridays.
Eighty-seven thousand, six-hundred hours.
Over five million minutes of life devoured.
Across oceans and high seas,
Three hundred and sixty degrees,
Crisscrossing our Earth,
Through melancholy and mirth,
To end up here,
On this point of lithosphere,
Where it all began,
…from where you ran.
And here you be,
The jaunting returnee,
To be as you were,
and have yesteryears reoccur.

I felt bemused,
Until reality suffused…
You didn't leave,
I misperceived,

You voyaged to the West,
To decompress,
It was me that ran,
From where it began,
You travelled for leisure,
I fled from displeasure,
You were sightseeing,
While I was fleeing,
You had adventures to tell,
I had memories to expel,
You left to return,
I watched those bridges burn.
I guess evolution,
Varies with revolutions,
How our lives contrast,
Now ten years have passed:
Three thousand, six hundred and forty-eight
days.
That's one hundred and twenty paydays.
Over two hundred and ninety billion seconds
To evolve and grow through life's lessons.

www.ingramcontent.com/pod-product-compliance
Lightning Source LLC
Chambersburg PA
CBHW051740130826
49812CB00033B/946
* 9 7 8 9 3 5 7 4 4 1 7 1 1 *